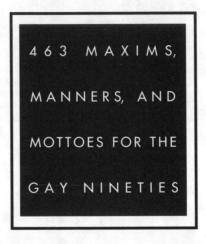

463 MAXIMS,

MANNERS, AND

MOTTOES FOR THE

GAY NINETIES

KEN HANES

A FIRESIDE BOOK Published by Simon&Schuster

New York London Toronto Sydney Tokyo Singapore

T H E

GAY GUYS

GUIDE TO

L I F E

F I R E S I D E
Rockefeller Center
1230 Avenue of the Americas, New York, NY 10020

FIRESIDE and colophon are registered trademarks of Simon & Schuster Inc.
Designed by Crowded House & Co.
Manufactured in the United States of America
10 9 8 7 6 5 4 3
Library of Congress Cataloging-in-Publication Data
Hanes, Ken.
The gay guys guide to life : 463 maxims, manners, and mottoes for the gay nineties /
Ken Hanes.
p.   cm.
"A Fireside book."
1. Gays—Quotations, maxims, etc. I. Title.
PN6084.G35H36   1994
305.9'06642—dc20   94-4055   CIP
ISBN 0-671-88356-9

ACKNOWLEDGMENTS

During the fall of 1992, Wayne Shimabukuro asked me to join him and a friend at a movie. I had plans, said no, and then changed my mind and showed up anyway. The dull movie was followed by a terrific bit of luck, because the friend Wayne introduced me to was Chase Langford. During the post-movie dinner, Chase mentioned a birthday present he had made for a friend of his—a collection of instructions about being gay. Within a week, Chase and I were on our way to writing this book. Unfortunately, Chase had to bow out of the project, but his spirit and presence still permeate this book.

In addition to Chase, I have many people to thank for their help. Charlotte Sheedy has been everything a writer could dream for in an agent. Elaine Pfefferblit and Laura Demansky at Poseidon Press initially helped get the project rolling, and Mitch Horowitz has been an insightful, supportive, helpful and friendly editor.

Plus, I give many thanks and hugs to the supportive friends who helped me through the process — Christopher Keenan, Eric Graham, Mary Bleier, Allan Hollingsworth and angel on earth Nina Brown.

INTRODUCTION

When I was nine years old, my mother took my hand and sat me next to her on the tattered couch in our den. Dad sat on my other side, so I was sandwiched between my parents, my thin knees and legs squashed together from their expansive adult thighs. Mom and Dad weren't touchy feely types. I knew not to mistake this strange closeness for affection. They must have thought I was going to bolt. I had no idea what I had done, and that made me want to bolt even more.

A serious talk from my parents usually concerned cleaning up after the dog in the backyard, so I was as interested as I was in my mom's chopped liver. Then Mom gave Dad one of *those* looks. Dad pulled down a slim book from the top corner of the built-in bookshelves that spanned the wall. He took a deep breath, then opened the book. A picture book? Please, I'm nine years old! But I was too apprehensive to protest. My parents went into their spiel. They basically said *men have this thing and women have that hole and he puts it you-know-where and a baby is made.* But guess what? Where to put you-know-what when a woman wasn't present was never mentioned. The sex-between-men chapter seemed to have gotten lost somewhere between reality and the publisher.

The limited scope of the obligatory birds-and-the-bees talk was not terribly destructive for me, because I doubt that any parent can truly teach their children about sex. Oh, they can explain how bodies work, the mechanics of copulation, types of birth control and how to avoid diseases. But when push comes to shove, they can't explain sex to you without . . . push coming to shove. You learn sex with another human being, not your parents. The absence of a chapter on gay sex didn't so much deprive me of the facts of gay *sex* as of the facts of gay *life*.

By facts of life, I'm not referring to the nitty-gritties of sexual activity. I mean the knowledge one accumulates with years and the wisdom that gets passed down from generation to generation. A mother shares her hard-earned secrets about life with her daughter. A father teaches his son what the boy needs to know to get through life. But this familial avenue of education dead-ends when it comes to gays and lesbians. About ten percent of the children in America don't get what they need, because their parents have nothing to teach them about being gay. The facts of gay life remain outside the sphere of most parents' knowledge. And for those few who do have an awareness of gay life, sharing that knowledge with their sons or daughters may be the last thing they want to do.

Not only do our parents often fail us in our education as gays; most of the other traditional avenues of education fall far short of our needs, too.

I never knew two men could date, because my older sister dated boys, my oldest brother dated girls and my other brother dated no one at all. Scratch siblings.

I've seen dozens of coming-of-age movies that Hollywood has churned out over the years, but not a single gay one. Scratch movies.

I've watched hundreds of sitcom episodes where I've followed characters through their first dates, first kisses, romances and marriages, but I can't remember a single image of a healthy gay relationship on TV. Scratch TV.

When I went off to college, no one gave me a little instruction book on how to accept my sexuality or how to come out. Scratch books.

There were no role models, no visible relationships, no media images, no school friends, nothing. I was on my own.

I craved guidance, but it's difficult to find advice on how to live our lives. The advice I found about being gay was all negative—pray, repress, resist, closet. More and more of us are unwilling to do that. Like millions of other gay men, I was hungry for insights into how to lead a positive, healthy life as a gay man.

I've grown from a teenager who didn't understand in tenth grade health class how two men could possibly transmit a venereal disease to . . . well . . . the writer of a book for gay men. I've learned a lot over the years, mostly through the ways we all learn as we grow older—

experiences, trial and error, friends and, of course, therapy. This is the book I wish someone had given to me.

At some point during the writing, I had to make two important decisions. The first was whether this book should be for both gay men and lesbians or only for gay men. I've decided to limit myself to gay men. While I understand that lesbians might appreciate an instruction book, I'm certainly the wrong person to write it. It would be presumptuous and unfair to include advice for lesbians. Guidance for lesbians should be provided by a lesbian.

The second decision proved more difficult to arrive at. Should every single bit of guidance here specifically apply to gay life? Reading through these pages, you'll notice that many of the instructions could apply to anyone—gay men, lesbians, bisexuals or even straights. At first, I had thought I would include only guidance that applied to gay men. If the instruction worked for heterosexuals, I wouldn't include it. But that approach began to feel both heterophobic and homophobic. Just because an instruction applied to heterosexuals, why should it be taken away from us? It was that old trap: I was defining gays by contrasting them with straights, as if advice applying to *them* couldn't apply to *us,* as if guidance had value only when applied exclusively to *us.* That made no sense. To be honest to myself and to honor our community, I decided to include any instruction I believed had value for gay men, independently of whether or not it applies to heterosexuals, lesbians or bisexuals.

While I hope others might enjoy and benefit from this book, *The Gay Guys Guide to Life* is about gay men and for gay men. It's our little instruction book.

1 Turn your love for men into art. Where do you think Michelangelo's *David* came from?

2 If people dislike you because you're gay, it's their problem. Refuse to let them make it yours.

3 Don't coif *before* your workout.

4 Explore your spiritual side. Look into Louise Hay, A Course in Miracles, the Metropolitan Community Church or other spiritual groups in your community.

5 Take an AIDS activist out to lunch.

6 The right wing loves to write letters, so we need to balance their exuberance. Include politicians on your letter writing list, right next to Mom and Aunt Edna.

7 Be a good uncle. Every child needs a gay role model.

8 If you're drunk, stay away from places that pierce or tattoo.

9 Slow dance with your man at Disneyland.

10 Never iron your underwear. Neatness has its limits.

11 If your neckline is lower than your nipples, don't bother. You're wasting cloth.

12 Beware of people who think you're gay because you haven't found the right woman.

13 Particularly beware of a woman who thinks she might be the right woman.

14 People come out on their own timetable. Support them wherever they are in the process. (Exception: public figures with an antigay agenda. Then outing is self-defense.)

15 If someone assumes you're straight, it's not your obligation to come out to them. It's your choice.

16 Next time at a party, skip the Wicked Witch of the West imitation. We've *all* seen it before.

17 As long as our culture makes coming out an act of civil disobedience, being gay will be a political statement. Accept, at least for now, that your sexuality has political ramifications.

18 Before you criticize queens, fairies or someone who acts "too queer," consider where we'd be without them.

19 When dating, do everything you can to keep the game-playing to a minimum. Once you instigate the game, someone's going to win and someone's going to lose.

20 Let yourself laugh as loud as you please. There's nothing more spirited than an odd laugh ripping through a crowd.

21 Loosen up. Being masculine doesn't mean being a statue. Wrists were made to bend.

22 Never dress more flamboyantly than Liberace.

23 Know it's okay if your fantasies aren't politically correct. They're only fantasies.

24 Practice intimacy.

25 The American system is based on tolerance. Don't let anyone convince you otherwise.

26 Date the names in your little black book.

27 Being a gay man does not mean ignoring the other gender. Let women into your life.

28 Know it's okay to laugh at yourself and your gayness. Humor heals.

29 If a guy says no, take the *no* at face value. If he's playing games, let him play alone.

30 Send back your Publishers' Clearinghouse sweepstakes form (or other magazine promotionals) without ordering. Include a note that says you'll start ordering when they start carrying gay and lesbian magazines.

31 Look for and identify role models (parents, friends, media figures) who have the type of relationship you want.

32 If you go to a Twelve-Step meeting, work the Steps, not the room.

33 Don't abuse Call Waiting. Your boyfriend doesn't have to hang up on whoever he's talking to just because it's you.

34 Don't forget Chicago. We may check in with fewer numbers than in New York, San Francisco or Los Angeles, but it's a good place to be gay.

35 If you own or manage a hair salon or interior design company, consider hiring a heterosexual man.

36 Develop your business networking with the same boundless energy that goes into your social networking.

37 This is *the* homophobic equation: *gay = sick, lonely and unhappy*. Challenge the mathematics.

38 Before you lend your boyfriend money, consider this formula. Maximum money you'll lend per month should equal the lesser of (a) the amount you can afford never to see again or (b) your monthly income, divided by 100, times the number of years you've been together.

39 Always keep your wallet stocked with business cards. You never know when you'll meet Mr. Right.

40 Know that there is no Mr. Right. Gay men looking for Mr. Right usually stay single.

41 If you don't think the government is doing enough to fight AIDS, make sure you are.

42 Know how to put on a condom correctly. If you're not sure, ask for assistance.

43 We grew up with heterosexuality used as a weapon against us. Be bigger than that. Don't use your sexuality as a weapon against straights.

44 Straights are often uncomfortable with public displays of our affection. Don't censor your behavior because of their insecurities, but still be respectful.

45 If a man puts on his running shoes when you say "I love you," consider that he might not be a guy worth investing your love in.

46 Date etiquette: Don't make a big deal about who pays for what on a date. If he wants to pay for both of you, say thank you. And don't think you have to lick his plate for it. If you pay for both of you, don't expect anything in return.

47 Check out the gay computer bulletin boards. It's a fun and unique way to meet guys.

48 Don't fake an orgasm. It's a lie.

49 When hugging a guy you like, let *him* let go. If he doesn't let go, it could be the start of something beautiful, or at least steamy.

50 When you're not sure if he's gay:

•Ask him how many times he's seen *The Wizard of Oz*. Over 6 times as an adult, add 3 gay probability points. If he starts reciting key scenes verbatim, add 10 gay probability points.

•Count his earrings. Over 4 total or over 2 in one ear, in a city with a population of less than 500,000, add 5 gay probability points. Over 6 total or over 4 in one ear, in a city with a population greater than 500,000, add 2 gay probability points.

•Check if he showers at the gym facing the wall or back to the wall. Back to the wall, add 2 gay probability points. Facing the wall, subtract 2 points.

•Check out his tattoos. Zero tattoos = no change in gay probability. A tattoo with a butterfly or flower, add 1 gay probability point. A tattoo with a woman's name, subtract 3 gay probability points. A tattoo with a man's name, add 20 gay probability points.

•Ask him if he's read Kitty Kelly's biography of Nancy Reagan. If he's read it, add 1 gay probability point. If he liked it, add 2. If he can quote from it, add 5.

51 Most people (whether straight or gay) consider sex a private activity. Expose people to your sexuality, not your sexual activity.

52 When you feel safe, hold hands or kiss in public. Honestly showing your affection, but not your sexual activity, is a type of activism.

53 Quit smoking. Cigarettes can hinder a guy's erection and decrease the amount of sperm in an ejaculation. Smokers with HIV develop AIDS twice as quickly as nonsmokers, and many tobacco companies contribute large amounts of money to homophobes like Jesse Helms. Besides, there are much better things than a cigarette to put in your mouth.

54   Don't forget that sexually transmitted diseases—like gonorrhea, syphilis and chlamydia—still exist. Watch out.

55   Don't make a purchase based on the salesman's pecs or smile.

56   Recycle. Exception: condoms, boyfriends and dental floss.

57 If you have AIDS, drink bottled water that's bacteria free.

58 Don't buy any clothing you'd be embarrassed to wash at a Laundromat.

59 Live your fantasy.

60 Ways to deal with a woman's come-ons: out yourself, avoid eye contact, run.

61 See Marlon Riggs's *Tongues Untied*.

62 See *Paris Is Burning*.

63 Mothers, fathers, veterans, presidents and even groundhogs have holidays. We deserve them, too. Celebrate gay and lesbian national holidays—National Coming Out Day, Gay and Lesbian Pride Week. They're ours.

64 Whenever *Newsweek, Time* or other national magazines publish an issue about gays or lesbians, buy it. Mainstream publishers need to know that gay covers sell.

65 Don't try to seduce a straight man. Unless he begs.

66 Tell the truth in your personal ads. Lying only wastes someone else's time.

67 Try wearing 501 jeans without underwear. This is known as freeballing.

68 Money talks. Use your dollars to support gay-friendly businesses.

69 As an adult, do the things you wanted to do as a child but were told you couldn't because they were "sissy."

70 Don't spend more than one week's salary on your Halloween costume.

71 Practice wearing those heels *before* Halloween.

72 When in Atlanta, check out the drag shows. Nobody does drag like a Southern queen.

73 Don't let a wedding ring on a finger confuse you. We love jewelry and sometimes get the fingers mixed up.

74 Don't let sports be only for the straight guys. If you like the game, play it.

75 Find a doctor you trust enough to be candid with. A doctor won't be much help if you have to hide things from him.

76 Limit how often you watch *Whatever Happened to Baby Jane?* Even the best of us could become Bette Davis.

77 When taking an aerobics class "just because the instructor's *so* cute," be extra careful warming up. The combination of irrational attraction and excessive exercise can easily lead to pulled muscles.

78 If you want to hang nude male photographs in your home, do it. It's your home.

79 Check out the gay Mardi Gras in Australia.

80 We wear one earring, straights start wearing one. We wear two, straights start wearing two. Heterosexual culture always steals our looks, ideas, words and styles. So copyright and patent whatever possible, and then get used to it.

81 Remember Mother's Day and Father's Day.

82 During a workout at the gym, wipe your sweat off the pad after finishing with a machine.

83 No matter how strong the attraction, *never* attempt to pick up an on-duty police officer.

84 When staying in a gay and lesbian bed-and-breakfast, don't think it's okay to be a nonstop partier simply because the place is gay and lesbian. Most people go to bed-and-breakfasts for romance, rest or seclusion.

85 If you are the victim of a bashing or hate crime, report it.

86 Working out's fine, but don't let your biceps become bigger than your head.

87 Learn how to laugh off verbal abuse.

88 Learn when something's too abusive to laugh off.

89 If a lesbian asks you for a sperm donation, don't take the request lightly. Think it through thoroughly.

90 Sure, we say we like tigers in bed. But don't maul. Few of us want scratches.

91 If you see a guy being bashed, don't look the other way. If you can't safely help him, call the police and get reinforcements.

92 Learn self-defense.

93 Carry a whistle if it'll make you feel safer.

94 Don't feel you can snap a photo of a guy just because he's good-looking. (Exception—at any Halloween celebration or gay pride festival, everyone's fair game for a photo.)

95 Get tested for HIV. Knowledge does equal power.

96 Cross-dress your Barbie and Ken.

97 Read *The Mayor of Castro Street: The Life and Times of Harvey Milk* by Randy Shilts.

98 Learn first aid.

99 Go to the Gay Games at least once, whether you're a sports fan or not.

100 Fill out a medical powers of attorney form to delineate who you want to care for you in case of an accident or illness.

101 Difficult times can bring out your best and worst. Make sure AIDS brings out the part you want.

102 If you own a business, donate your products or services to gay and lesbian political groups and their fundraisers.

103 When you get home from a vacation, don't tell your boyfriend how hot all the guys were *there*.

104 If someone verbally harasses you (*hey, faggot*), don't respond to the taunt unless you're prepared to fight back.

105 If you choose to be monogamous, know that keeping a sex life exciting can be difficult—but it can be done. Be prepared for an exciting challenge.

106 Never read your boyfriend's journal.

107 Have pride, but also have the humility to admit when you're full of hot air.

108 Libido and performance change with age, health and moods. Don't beat yourself up for it.

109 Beware of homophobic remarks. (Gays make them, too.)

110 Throughout history, all plagues have ended. Stand fast. AIDS is not forever.

111 When passing a garage sale that benefits an AIDS organization, buy something even if you don't need it.

112 Don't expect your boyfriend to be a mind reader and know what you're thinking or feeling. Help him.

113 Request that your public library carry gay and lesbian books.

114 Swim nude every now and then.

115 Don't leave an outgoing message on your answering machine that you wouldn't want your grandma to hear.

116 Don't leave sexually explicit messages on anyone else's answering machine unless you know they want them.

117 All the world's a stage. Dress the part you are playing.

118 Dress against type. It keeps them guessing.

119 Don't use your roommate's condoms. Few things are worse or more dangerous than being revved up, then finding your roommate's used all your condoms.

120 When you ignore the above, replace the condoms you borrow. Within twenty-four hours.

121 Always be your best, even when you're alone. Remember, you're your best audience.

122 Make weird sounds and faces when you are alone. Sometimes we need practice being ourselves.

123 We all don't *have* to live in a gay area. Don't ghettoize yourself unless that's what you really want.

124 If your boyfriend asks you to hold him, don't ask why. Just do it.

125 Don't rent videos from a store that doesn't carry gay and lesbian films.

126 Balance every night at Club Fuck with a night at home.

127 Don't give away your rights, and don't take away anyone else's.

128 Some men will lie if they want to get laid badly enough. Beware. *Always* assume your partner is HIV positive.

129 If you hang out with your friends only in bars, you'll never really get to know them. Go someplace where you can talk easily.

130 If you want to fall in love, focus on being lovable.

131 Attitude is a prison. Break free.

132 When on your first few dates with a man, don't bring up your ex-boyfriends unless the guy specifically asks. He probably doesn't want to know.

133 Introduce your friends to one another. Build a community.

134 Try saying hello to a cute guy without checking out his basket. Just once.

135 Homophobic laws may prevent us from marrying, but we can still create our own ceremonies. 'Til death do us part.

136 Don't do something just because you think it's butch. Do it because you like it.

137 Only call a 976 or 900 number that charges by the day or hour, not the minute.

138 Gay rights are your rights. Do everything you can to support and create them.

139 The fight against AIDS is a long haul. Take care of yourself to minimize burnout.

140 Don't be shy buying condoms.

141 Involve your friends with the gay community Invite them to club meetings, art openings and charity events. This goes for your straight friends, too.

142 Be aware that by misleading people into thinking that you are straight, you're telling them there's something wrong with being gay.

143 Never let these be visible in your home: condoms, lube, pornography, your diary. Keep them in drawers and cabinets.

144 Every now and then, discuss with your partner how your relationship is going.

145 Write love letters to the man you love, even if you live together.

146 Use the *Gay and Lesbian Yellow Pages* first.

147 Learn the difference between lust and love.

148 Start a gay and lesbian student group at your school if you don't already have one.

149 Read the Lambda Book Award winners each year.

150 When meeting a potential boyfriend, think about what you have to offer him, not only about what he has that you want.

151 Don't discriminate against heterosexuals.

152 When you're dancing up a sweat, don't slime innocent bystanders. Not everyone wants a sweat shower.

153 If you have AIDS, don't think your doctor knows all the answers. He or she doesn't.

154 If you have AIDS, keep up on recent research. Become an expert. No one's as interested in your future as you are.

Subscribe to
 AIDS Treatment News
 P.O. Box 411256
 San Francisco, CA 94141
 (800) 873-2812

155   Don't flirt with a woman who thinks you're straight. It's a mindfuck.

156   Never seduce a guy who doesn't want to be.

157   Don't let yourself be seduced when you don't want to be.

158   If you have AIDS, be wary of people who believe having HIV or AIDS means you have to die.

159 Always help a person coming out. Until society changes, we all need guidance.

160 Take precautions against insects when having outdoor sex.

161 Don't work on pickup lines. Develop your spontaneity and charm.

162 If it feels good, don't do it until you're sure it's safe.

163 Write your elected officials and let them know how you feel. When writing Al Gore, include a picture of yourself and your phone number.

164 Define your anniversary—the day you met, your first date, the day you made a commitment.

165 Think twice—no, three times—before agreeing to let a man you're attracted to move in as your roommate.

166 Don't give him a sexually graphic card, present or cake unless you're certain he'll appreciate it.

167 Political T shirts are great, but don't let that be your only political expression. Get involved.

168 Maintain your health insurance.

169 Stay off the dance floor of a club if you have a bottle or glass. They almost always spill or break.

170 Learn from the mistakes that straight men made in the seventies. Don't confuse masculine with macho.

171 If you're angry or depressed about the world's homophobia, don't stew. Find a positive outlet for your anger (like political activism). It's good for your mental health and good for social change.

172 Share child care.

173 If you have AIDS, eat defensively. As T cells decline, a person becomes much more susceptible to illness caused by bacteria in food.

174 Don't name your cat Ms. Kitty, Big Mama, Pussy Galore or any other name women might find offensive.

175 Be reckless in love but not in sex.

176 In a waiting room for HIV test results, don't make jokes. Everyone's on edge, and someone will definitely not appreciate it.

177 Don't let anyone saddle you with a label you don't like for the man in your life (husband, boyfriend, lover, partner, significant other). If you want labels, choose your own.

178 Demand that your parents treat you and your lover just as they treat your siblings and their spouses (assuming that's good).

179 Know that coming out is not a panacea. All your problems won't miraculously disappear.

180 Respect people's confidentiality. Don't repeat what you hear in a Twelve-Step meeting or group therapy.

181 Try out a men's support group.

182 Consider couples counseling before you break up.

183 If you're sure you want to break up, consider couples counseling to help you break up.

184 Falling in love with your therapist may be a cliche—but it's still a real danger. Choose a therapist you're sure is ethical.

185 Don't ever have sex with your therapist.

186 When ending a relationship, do your best to have a formal sense of closure.

187 If you find straight people boring, look at the parts of yourself you're closing down because you're around straights.

188 If you find women boring, look at the feminine traits you're not letting out.

189 If you find other gays boring, look at the parts of yourself you don't like.

190 If you find yourself boring, get a perm, take a trip or find a new job. In other words, shake up your life. (But read 191 first.)

191 Before you dye your hair, wax or shave your body, use makeup or make other cosmetic adjustments, ask some friends for their opinions. Sometimes we do more harm than good.

192 Remember, acceptance is acknowledging our sexuality as something God-given. Self-love is thanking God for the gift.

193 If you're accusing someone of homophobia, make sure you're not projecting your own.

194 Choose your therapist carefully. He or she doesn't have to be gay or lesbian, but make sure they're gay-affirmative.

195 Gays can be assholes, too. Don't think you have to like a guy just because he's gay.

196 For a special occasion, ask a friend (or hire a chef) to come to your home to prepare and serve a romantic dinner for you and your boyfriend. Throw in a masseur while you're at it.

197 Complain to newspapers and magazines that don't accept same-gender ads in their personal section.

198 Don't give bisexuals a hard time for being bi. They can't control their attractions to both genders anymore than you can control your attraction to one.

199 Explore tantric sex.

200 Live your relationship like a Twelve-Step program: plan for the future but take it day by day.

201 Take caution before criticizing your lover.

202 Take even more caution before criticizing your lover's mother.

203 Honor older gay men and lesbians. They've had to live through a hostile world most of us will never know.

204 Don't compare your new boyfriend to your old one, either positively or negatively.

205 When you ignore the above and do compare the new and the old, don't let either find out.

206 Consider mediation before litigation. The courts can be very user-unfriendly to gays and lesbians.

207 If you have a type, at least once date a guy who's *not* your type.

208 Watch *Longtime Companion*.

209 Hospitals can be creepy, but don't abandon your friends who are in one. Let friendship win.

210 If your therapist mentions reparative therapy, run as fast as you can.

211 If you have the flu (or some other contagious ailment), stay away from people with AIDS.

212 Beware of men who use glow-in-the-dark condoms.

213 Bash back. Fire deserves fire.

214 Don't bash back. Fire needs water.

215 The world can be violently antigay. Whatever your choice about bashing or not, be prepared.

216 If you depend on dishing for fun, stay home and do the dishes. Adults who think that hurting someone else is fun are not adults. We of all people should have learned that by now.

217 When coming out or introducing your boyfriend to your parents, do it on neutral turf.

218 Never wear more rings (ear, nose, nipple, cock or otherwise) than you can get through a metal detector at an airport.

219 Give generously to charity. If you don't have enough income to donate money to charity (or even if you do), donate your time. An hour spent with a person with AIDS can be invaluable for both you and them.

220 Give *Is the Homosexual My Neighbor?* by Letha Scanzoni and Virginia Ramey Mollenkott to family and friends who are bothered by your homosexuality because of Christian views.

221 Learn how to combat fundamentalist attacks on your sexuality.

222 Some people say gays shouldn't have children. So what? Make your own choice about kids. There are ways.

223 Learn to cook. It's easy and makes your home more of a home.

224 Remember, some of the best weekends are spent at home.

225 Take a nonsexual shower with your boyfriend every now and then. And scrub his back.

226 We all share *the* gay experience, but everyone has his own gay experience. Don't stereotype us.

227 Try not to fear romance.

228 Try not to fear commitment.

229 Try not to fear change.

230 Don't call women bitches, cunts or fish. Being derogatory toward women only reflects a lack of self-esteem—not to mention it's downright rotten. Showing sensitivity toward women is a virtue.

231 After introducing your boyfriend and your parents for the first time, do not leave them alone with one another for the next few hours—or maybe even days—unless everyone agrees to it.

232 If your definition of safer sex differs from your partner's, go with whatever is more stringent.

233 Don't be self-conscious. Risk your reputation for the sake of making a joke. Laughter overrides image.

234 When you connect with a man's body, don't forget his heart and soul.

235 Gay liberation is not about us having the freedom to adopt the bad habits of straights. Think higher. Transcend.

236 When you're with someone—boyfriend, date, friend or otherwise—be with them. Don't let your roving eyes take you away from the person you're with.

237 Preventing homophobia begins with children. Teach acceptance and respect.

238 When in a relationship, work on the friendship. As passion eases, friendship can bloom.

239 When visiting Los Angeles, make out with a guy in the Hollywood Hills from a vantage point that has a view of the city.

240 Some gay men are quite adept at separating sex from love. Allow yourself to integrate the two.

241 Use sex to express love in addition to fulfilling physical needs.

242 When in Los Angeles, take a look at the new Gay and Lesbian Community Services Center building— the largest gay and lesbian building in the world. It's hard not to feel a tinge of pride.

243 Relationships take work. Get busy.

244 Never date anyone who turns out to be more work than fun.

245 Don't try to change your partner. But give him plenty of space and encouragement to change when he wants to.

246 Give pleasure. Accept pleasure. It's that easy.

247 Work out to feel good, not to make people feel good about you.

248 When your boyfriend needs time apart, be gracious and give it to him.

249 Remember, no situation (including AIDS) is so grave that it's not fit for a joke. (See *Diseased Pariah News* for proof.)

250 But remember, no situation is so simple that it's okay to be insensitive while making a joke.

251 And remember, no joke is so funny that anyone will suffer if they don't hear it.

252 Meeting men can be difficult. Have group dinners, parties or events so you can introduce your friends to one another.

253 Matchmaking is a dangerous business. Don't do it carelessly, but if your instinct tells you there's potential, go ahead and fix the guys up. And then step back and take cover.

254 Because we couple with the same sex, we don't have to contend with society's definitions of gender roles in a relationship. Define your own role or choose whether you even want to have a role.

255 Don't leave a used condom lying around if you have pets.

256 At the very least, try to be out in your own home. Having to hide at that level is the ultimate repression.

257 Understand how to strengthen your immune system.

258 Consider including a gay and lesbian organization in your will.

259 When visiting Copenhagen, hold hands or smooch in public. No one will care.

260 Being a sophisticated, urbane gay man is not in conflict with nature. Learn to appreciate the outdoors.

261 Ask for what you want in bed.

262 Don't be afraid to say no to something your partner asks of you in bed.

263 Yank your friends out of the bars and gyms and insist on some other activity that isn't their norm. They may grumble at first, but in the end they'll probably thank you. If they don't thank you, get some new friends.

264 If a guy asks you out and you're not interested, be clear. Sometimes, it's hard to hear a *no* unless the word is said strongly.

265 Don't push people with AIDS into a little box and treat them differently.

266 If you're a person with AIDS, don't let anyone else push you into a box. Let people know how you expect to be treated.

267 Don't finish the last piece of his birthday cake without asking.

268 Don't hide your gayness from children.

269 If you're a person with AIDS, hang onto your power. Friends and enemies alike often try to take control.

270 The line between flirting and sexual harassment is thin. *Always* make sure you're not overstepping a boundary.

271 Any cruise that embarrasses the cruisee is over-done. Slow down.

272 Any cruise that causes neck or back strain is over-done. Have control.

273 Don't be ashamed about having a therapist. Therapy is an act of self-love.

274 If a guy tells you he's hung, don't believe it until you've done your own inspection.

275 Don't tell a guy you're hung unless you're willing to let him do his own inspection.

276 If you're having sex with a guy and he can't get it up, don't make a big deal about it. And there's no need to tell him how that never happens to you.

277 When visiting New York, oh hell, just do it all.

278 Keep a diary. And for God's sake make it juicy.

279 Don't assume it's okay to wear his clothing. Always ask.

280 Nothing's wrong with no-strings-attached sex. It's a personal choice. But remember, if one of you gets hurt, then a string was attached (and one often is).

281 Create and build a family of friends that will last your lifetime.

282 Don't believe in "gay time." Late is late and rude is rude.

283 Sex isn't everything in a relationship, but at least *try* to be a good lover.

284 Don't take niceness in a guy for granted. It's a rare commodity.

285 When housesitting for a friend, never leave another guy's underwear under the owner's bed.

286 The gay and lesbian vote is huge and powerful. Let's use it not only to our advantage but to make this a better place for *everyone*.

287 Strongly support another's rights. Liberation is liberation.

288 Share your creativity with the man in your life: write him a poem, sing him a song, paint him a picture.

289 Learn to navigate the map of your own body.

290 Touch yourself as intimately as you want others to.

291 Read at least one national gay and lesbian magazine.

292 Read your local gay and lesbian newspaper.

293 If you don't have a local gay and lesbian newspaper, get busy.

294 Keep a journal of your coming out process. It could be invaluable later on.

295 Learn to see beyond a man's looks.

296 Don't say "I love you" unless you mean it.

297 Say "I love you" a lot once you *do* mean it.

298 Some men are in the market for a husband. Some men are looking for company for only a few hours. We have different needs and desires. Be clear about what you want.

299 There is no cure for homosexuality because there is nothing to cure. But there is a cure for homophobia. Work on it.

300 Homophobia is fear and ignorance. So educate, don't attack. But remember, it's not your job to educate the ineducable.

301 Don't overdo it in front of the bathroom mirror. There's a point of diminishing returns. Simplicity and casualness win out over heavy primping any day.

302 Know that hiding your sexuality is usually more trouble than it's worth.

303 Learn the gay looks, whether to use them or avoid
them.

•Gay Look #1: *Politico.* Hair extremes (long or short).
Piercing and/or tattoos. Goatees, Vandykes and/or thin, angular sideburns. Wear mid-length shorts whenever possible. T-shirts with slogans. Grunge acceptable.

•Gay Look #2: *Boy Toy.* Gym body, often waxed or shaved.
Precision haircut. Tight T-shirts or loose tank tops. Crisp tan line or absolutely no tan line.

•Gay Look #3: *Leather Man.* Wears only skins—his own and a cow's. Shoes, belts and watchbands not indicative of look. Piercing and/or tattoos. Mustaches common.

•Gay Look #4: *(Radical) Faerie.* Neohippie plus some. Knee-length flowing skirt (no dresses). Large jewelry. Facial hair. Sandals or boots. T-shirts with slogans.

304 Leave your man surprise goodies in the fridge.

305 In matters of love and sex, we're at our most vulnerable. So always take care in these situations.

306 When you get a pubic hair stuck in your mouth, be graceful. A spitting fit is not erotic.

307 If the energy is right, make your move on a guy.

308 If the energy isn't right, don't push it.

309 Give flowers.

310 Know that being gay and spiritual is not a contradiction.

311 Know that being gay and voting for an antigay candidate is a contradiction.

312 In bars, you party with acquaintances. Make some of them friends by inviting them into your home. Bars = Acquaintances. Home = Friends.

313 Have your safer sex discussion before the heat of the moment. Once you're turned on, it's difficult to discuss anything.

314 Society has built a huge cage around us because of our sexuality. Push the bars aside.

315 The first time you meet your boyfriend's family, don't kiss his father hello.

316 Notice the companies that advertise in gay and lesbian publications.

317 Avoid oil-based lubricants. Some oils eat through latex.

318 The *Kama Sutra* says honey is an aphrodisiac. Give it a try. If it's not true, at least you'll have a sweet, wet, sticky evening.

319 Go see a gay men's chorus. Any of them.

320 Quit bickering with your boyfriend in front of friends. Unless it's part of your shtick.

321 If bickering is part of your shtick, ask your friends if it annoys them or not.

322 Shower your boyfriend with little surprises as often as you think of them. (And try to think of them often.)

323 Don't hire an employee because he's good-looking.

324 Don't *not* hire an employee because he's unattractive.

325 When you're not sure, pursue a guy just for the learning experience, if nothing else.

326 Know that carrying a condom in your wallet or glove compartment is not juvenile or sleazy. If you have the need, then it's practical. If you don't have the need, then who cares?

327   While people are dating, their feelings for each other often develop on different timetables. When you're not at the same place, be willing to talk about it.

328   Smile at a stranger (and be subtle checking out his buns once he's passed).

329   Most of us have sustained huge wounds because of our sexuality. Heal yourself. It's a gift for future generations of gay men and lesbians.

330 Sex releases chemicals in your body that reduce pain and induce euphoria. When you have a headache, consider having sex instead of avoiding it.

331 Most of us grew up with little or no support for our gay core. Make up for that now: be extra supportive of your gay brothers and lesbian sisters.

332 Have compassion for your friends who aren't out yet. Remember, we were all in the closet once.

333 Don't vacation exclusively at gay resorts. Palm Springs, Fire Island, Rehoboth Beach, Provincetown, Key West, Russian River, Saugatuck—they're all great places, but there's more to the world.

334 Hang out with people of different ages and lifestyles. People unlike you can enrich your life.

335 Avoid animal-skin condoms. They don't prevent HIV transmission.

336 Bathroom etiquette: don't use each other's razors.

337 Don't use sex as a weapon.

338 Don't be a prick tease. Unless your lover likes it.

339 Cruising has etiquette. Stay out of public restrooms. It's illegal, unsanitary, and is the worst PR for the gay community imaginable.

340 Give your boyfriend an unrequested backrub.

341 Create an alternative family, but don't let that push you away from your biological family.

342 Know this: to fuck is human, to make love divine.

343 If all gays and lesbians recycled, we'd reduce the world's garbage by ten percent. Get to it.

344 If you're cruising someone and he doesn't respond, then drop it. Not all guys are into cruising.

345 Learn to put on a partner's condom with your right hand. Then your left hand. Then your mouth.

346 Understand your legal and civil rights.

347 Make rules with yourself about sex with married men (or co-workers or neighbors) *before* the opportunity arises.

348 Sexism and homophobia are flip sides of the same sick coin. Fight both.

349 Think twice before liposuction.

350 Self-check your testicles for lumps on a routine basis.

351 When telling a dirty joke, go for it, but be sensitive to those within earshot.

352 Give gay businesses the first opportunity to serve you.

353 Moisturize. Taking care of your skin is not feminine.

354 Some of us criticize others for anonymous sex and sleeping around. Some of us criticize others for being monogamous or homebodies. Straights have judged us for years about what we do in bed. Get past the judgment. We're all different.

355 Participate in the current fad only if you enjoy it. Don't do it for image.

356 Gay standards of physical beauty are oppressive. Ease up. Everyone will be happier and lighter.

357 Challenge people on their racist, sexist and homophobic jokes.

358 Have a will. Inheritance laws were made for heterosexuals. Having a will delineates your choices.

359 Tell your lover what gives you the most sexual pleasure.

360 Don't demean your lover in public or private. Others already demean us enough.

361 Abolish sexual guilt, but accept sexual responsibility.

362 Consider writing and signing a relationship contract when you're ready to commit. This can include not only financial matters but behavioral too, such as what sexual behavior is acceptable in or out of the relationship, a date night a set number of times a month, or even who will take out the trash.

363 Listen to your sexual desires.

364 Write to networks and studios about the TV shows and movies that reflect (positively or negatively) on the gay experience.

365 Beware of the color white, especially for sofas, carpets and cashmere sweaters. Cum leaves a nasty stain.

366 Believe it or not, there's more to a guy's bedroom than his bed. Ask him about his books, his desk, that chair, that rug. Remember, this is his life you're climbing into.

367 Keep your sex life exciting. Some tips:
- share your fantasies with your partner
- give your partner his fantasy as a gift
- try edible body paints
- experiment (safely)
- vary the types of condoms you use
- explore different lubes
- vary the time and place you have sex
- put the cantaloupe in the microwave for a couple of minutes

368 Don't intentionally try to make someone jealous, even if he deserves it. Especially when he deserves it.

369 Humor and sex mix well. Go ahead and laugh in bed.

370 When buying a house with your lover, try to find a master bathroom that has two sinks. This could be a key ingredient to a successful relationship.

371 Go hiking and camping. It's good for the soul, and you'll look great in those boots.

372 Falling in love rarely happens without taking some emotional risks. If you want love, allow yourself to take the risk.

373 If your parents feel guilty because you're gay, help them redefine their thoughts so it's not a question of anybody's fault. Buy them books to read on the subject. Direct them toward P-FLAG (Parents and Friends of Lesbians and Gays).

374 Be creative with dates:
- take him to a tarot reader
- climb a mountain and count stars
- videotape each other doing something nonsexual
- watch cartoons
- read to each other

The possibilities are endless.

375 Monogamy and nonmonogamy are personal choices. Do whatever makes your relationship work. But whatever the choice, mutual honesty is essential.

376 Beware of dates who look in the mirror more than they look at you.

377 Remember, being out of the closet is easier than being in. Ask anyone who's been both places.

378 *Never* try to coerce a guy to do something that's outside his guidelines for safer sex.

379 As a group, gays are quite photogenic. Take pictures.

380 Send copies of photos to friends.

381 Think twice about fighting the battle of the hair-line with a rug. A toupee can scare off more guys than a bald head. If you're uncomfortable with losing your hair, work on your smile.

382 Expose your straight friends and family to the diversity of the gay community in a proud way. Remember, our diversity is a strength, not a weakness.

383 Never flush a condom down the toilet. It can clog the pipes.

384 When bringing your boyfriend home to meet your parents, decide *in advance* what behavior (kissing, holding hands) is acceptable in front of Mom and Dad and what is not.

385 Consider courtship instead of going to bed on the first date.

386 As a gay man, make sure you have:
- an answering machine
- a clear understanding of safer sex
- a bountiful selection of condoms, even if you don't plan on using them
- control over your gag reflex

387 Don't avoid old sex partners when you see them. Having had sex with someone is not an excuse for the cold shoulder (no matter how terrible the sex was). Unless, of course, the person was an abusive asshole.

388 Don't smoke around a person with AIDS.

389 Take some time off from sex every now and then. Don't let it become an addiction.

390 There is Jewish humor, there is Black humor, there is WASP humor, there is Catholic humor, and there is gay humor. Embrace it.

391 Words to the Wise. Never believe these assertions:
- "Don't worry. I'll pull out."
- "He's only my roommate."
- "We broke up last week."
- "I won't cum in your mouth."
- "I'm over him. Really."
- "Nine inches. I've measured."
- "It won't hurt that much."

392 Not having children often makes gays ignore things like retirement, financial security and long-term planning. Think ahead.

393 Love your own body. It allows true pleasure through the door.

394 In social situations, be open and friendly to everyone, not only the men you're attracted to.

395 Don't push a friend to lose his virginity if he's not ready.

396 Your chromosomes may determine your gender, but don't let your gender determine your activities. If you like sewing, then sew.

397 Beware of bars and clubs where you have to pass through a metal detector to get in.

398 Beware of a man who triggers a metal detector. Or if you're into that sort of thing, get his phone number—especially if he has to excuse himself to the bathroom to remove the offending metal.

399 Be wary of western medicine and its profit motive.

400 Remember gay couples' anniversaries.

401 Make an extra effort for your gay organization to include people of all colors, ages and walks of life.

402 Bigger is better when it comes to chocolate bars. But remember, dicks are a matter of personal taste.

403 If there is a big difference between your lover's income and yours, perhaps some expenses can be handled on a percentage basis instead of splitting them equally. Work out some sort of solution. Do not let the imbalance play a destructive role in your relationship.

404 Remember, clones let fashion style them. An individual is self-styled.

405 Don't worry if you can't accessorize. It's easy to find friends who can.

406 Initiate sex. Your partner can't always turn on the ignition.

407 Seek romantic advice, but go ahead and ignore it.

408 On one of your visits to San Francisco, stay away from the gay bars and clubs. There's a whole city outside the bars.

409 Don't get hung up about whether homosexuality is genetic, environmental or a choice. Homosexuality simply is.

410 Shop at malls as a last resort.

411 Know that you can never be too kind or loving to your boyfriend.

412 Toilet etiquette: Women usually dislike the toilet seat left up. Men usually think it's a hassle to place the seat up and down. So compromise. If you have a female roommate, leave both the toilet seat and the toilet cover down. That way, the burden is shared equally. (But if you don't have a female roommate, leave the toilet seat up. It's more butch.)

413 If your friend or lover is living with AIDS, don't try to control his life. He must make his own decisions.

414 If your friend or lover is dying of AIDS, don't control his death. Let him die as he wishes.

415 If your friend or lover is living or dying with AIDS, make sure you find support for yourself. It can be hard on you, too.

416 Don't use the term *straight-acting* to describe yourself. It's homophobic to assume that acting masculine is straight and acting feminine is gay.

417 Being HIV negative or HIV positive is creating two very different experiences for gay men. Try not to let our serostatus separate us.

418 Everybody seems to have a set amount of time you're supposed to wait before calling a guy after the first date. Unfortunately, no one seems to agree on how long. So call whenever you want. If it's too soon and he freaks out, or too long and he's insulted, let him go.

419 Beware of a big threat to gay relationships: *two* male egos.

420 If you're on a date with a guy, and the waiter is rude to you because you're gay, leave one penny for a tip.

421 Don't tell anyone who has AIDS that you understand what they're going through. Unless you have AIDS too, you probably don't understand.

422 If you have AIDS and someone tells you he understands what you're going through, try not to explode. He probably means well.

423 Vote. Always.

424 Don't stretch the truth. Six inches is six inches, not eight and a half.

425 Growing up, we weren't listened to by others. We didn't listen to ourselves. Now, make an effort to listen to what your gay and lesbian friends are saying.

426 If it makes you feel sexy, wear it.

427 If you want a long-term relationship, focus on what is lasting. If you continually let your flings destroy a relationship, maybe there's something you want more than a relationship.

428 Please, have more than one cum rag.

429 Don't withhold sex to punish your boyfriend when you're angry.

430 Don't use sex as a reward to get your boyfriend to do something he doesn't want to do. Manipulation usually backfires.

431 Know that you're in good physical shape when you're aerobically fit, not only when you have big muscles.

432 At the end of a date, saying "I'll call you" when you won't is chickenshit. Don't do it.

433 Support and encourage gay and lesbian writers and artists.

434 If you can afford it, buy a VCR with four heads. The freeze-frame image will be much clearer.

435 Don't partner with a guy who has a dog unless you love dogs, too. If you do partner with him, be prepared for second place.

436 Before traveling to another country, get a gay guide. You'd be surprised what's legal or illegal in some countries.

437 Always wear shoes in sex clubs.

438 If you want to be buried with your partner, make the necessary arrangements now.

439 Remember, plastic surgery and implants may help you look better, but as soon as the gossip mill gets wind of your modifications, you'll lose points. Improvements can easily become detriments.

440 Know this: A pec is but a pec. A dick is but a dick. But a man with true heart is a treasure.

441 Gay pride is good, but don't let it separate you from straights.

442 Learn to be ambidextrous in sex. That way when you get bored with the right hand, you can try the left.

443 You don't have to accept anything less because you are gay. Don't expect anything more, either.

444 Don't let anyone pressure you into sex if you're not interested.

445 Go easy on the cologne. Not everybody wants the wafts of your cologne to fill their room.

446 Lobby your elected officials to support your rights. Hold them to all promises they make to our community.

447 Don't penny-pinch when it comes to your health.

448 Take the time to write notes and letters to your friends, even when they live in the same city. We love mail.

449 If possible, try to be friends with your ex's.

450 When you fall in love, don't abandon your friends.

451 When you fall in love, don't drag your friends into the drama.

452 Remember that your true love muscle is your heart.

453 As Bonnie Raitt says, "Don't advertise your man." Someone else might buy.

454 Sing the praises of your man. If you don't, he'll find someone else who will.

455 An orgasm can last sixty seconds (if you're lucky). Love can last a lifetime. Set priorities.

456 Seek pleasure, but don't let it rule your life.

457 Learn gay history. It's our history.

458 Don't be so focused on a guy's dick. There's often a person attached to it you might not like so much.

459 When visiting your family's home with your boyfriend, discuss the sleeping arrangement with your parents *in advance*.

460 Take a chance and slip the waiter your phone number.

461 Think twice before piercing yourself. Go to a professional.

462 Be in the moment with your boyfriend. Your relationship will benefit.

463 Stop worrying about eating quiche. People will tell you stupid maxims all the time. Have the insight to ignore advice that your gut tells you is wrong (including anything in this book).

Dear Reader,

If you have advice that you feel would be valuable to other gay men, and you would like me to share it with other readers, please write. Serious, humorous, political, campy, New Age, politically correct or incorrect—anything goes, as long as it pertains to gay men.

I look forward to hearing from you.

Ken Hanes
Gay Guys Guide to Life
6766-G Wrightsville Ave., Suite 193
Wilmington, NC 28403

Ken Hanes is a playwright and director
who lives in Venice, California.